THE HERO'S

JOURNEY

OF THE GAY

& LESBIAN

MORMON

THE HERO'S JOURNEY OF THE GAY & LESBIAN MORMON

by

Carol Lynn Pearson

Pivot Point Books
Walnut Creek • 2012

The Hero's Journey of the Gay and Lesbian Mormon was printed on acid-free paper and meets the permanence of paper requirememnts of the American National Standard for Information Sciences. This book was composed, printed, and bound in the United States of America.

16 15 14 13 12   8 7 6 5 4 3 1

Application has been made for registration and placement in the Library of Congress.

ISBN: 0-96388-527-8

For Gerald
always a Seeker

Joseph Campbell (1904-1987) is perhaps the pre-eminent mythologist of our time. The author of *Hero With a Thousand Faces* and many other works, Campbell won popular recognition for his collaboration with Bill Moyers in the remarkable 1988 PBS series, "The Power of Myth."

His lifelong passion for mapping the cohesive and seemingly universal threads in mythology, particularly the archetype of the hero, has strongly influenced modern culture. Filmmaker George Lucas credits Campbell's influence on his *Star Wars* films, as do the creators of *The Lion King* and numerous other movies and plays.

Can the entire human race, as Campbell suggests, be seen as reciting a single story of great spiritual importance? Is each of us called to be a hero in our own story? And are there steps we can discern that might help us make more sense of the journey?

I have come to specialize in the stories of the gay and lesbian members of our Mormon Tribe, who often are made to feel that their life story is a shameful one, or at least a lesser one. But what if, in fact, their calling can more truthfully be seen to have the value and the power of a Hero's journey?

Even though this story is set in Mormondom, it is, of course, applicable to gay people of any Tribe.

And to all of us, Campbell challenges:

The modern hero ... who dares to heed the call ... cannot, indeed must not, wait for his community to cast off its slough of pride, fear, rationalized avarice, and sanctified misunderstanding. "Live," Nietzsche says, "as though the day were here." It is not society that is to guide and save the creative hero, but precisely the reverse.

In the following story, the portions in italics are direct quotes from Joseph Campbell, with slight grammatical changes.

Step One

THE
ORDINARY
WORLD

You were a gift to the Tribe, the Mormon Tribe. And the Tribe was a gift to you. It kept you safe and warm. By the fire the Elders taught you of God, of goodness, of the divinity that pulsed in your heart, warming you like embers, sometimes like flames. The Elders drew in the sand the straight and narrow way that you must walk if you are to please God and return to his presence.

You learned very early what God and the Tribe expect of everyone. You knew we are on this earth to have joy. You knew the roles that had been assigned. You knew that boys become men who become leaders. You knew that girls become women who marry and have children. You knew this would happen because women and men fall in love with one another and it feels like a beautiful and a right thing and the future of the Tribe depends upon it. You knew that one day you too would follow this path and that God and the Tribe would continue to smile on you.

But ...

Step Two

THE CALL TO
ADVENTURE

J oseph Campbell:

*Look around, sister, brother of the Home Tribe.
Times are bad and the country all around seems
lifeless. The people grow weak before our eyes.
Someone must go out beyond the familiar terri-
tory. A figure emerges from the campfire smoke,
pointing to you. Yes, you have been chosen as
a Seeker and called to begin a new quest, an
adventure in which the only sure thing is that
you'll be changed. You're uneasy.*

"Me?" you ask fearfully.

"Not you alone," comes the reply from the
Wise One. "Many sooner or later will be called

to a special path. You are called to be a Seeker in a particular way, and if you say yes to the calling and succeed in your venture you will become a Hero. The Tribe is badly in need of Heroes, even though many in the Tribe would sacrifice your growth for your safety. This is what we call paradox. Listen."

You hear the drumbeat that you have heard all your life. But then it changes. You look around and realize that no one else seems to hear it the way you do. You say to yourself–

"There's something odd about me."

Then it becomes clear. "I am a boy and I like boys the way I'm told I should like girls."

Or–

"I am a girl and I like girls the way I'm told I should like boys."

And–

"This can't be right. There's a word for it and the word is *homosexual*. It's not a good word. There's something wrong with me!"

Step Three

REFUSAL
OF THE CALL

Joseph Campbell:

Some hesitate, some are tugged at by families who fear for your lives and don't want you to go. You hear people mutter that the journey is fool-hardy, doomed from the start. You feel fear constricting your breathing and making your heart race. Should you stay with the Home Tribe? Are you cut out to be a Seeker?

"No!" you think as you pull the blanket tight and shut your eyes. "I don't want to be different. I want to be like everyone else!"

You listen to the words of your family as they speak of the feelings you secretly have. It is clear that those feelings are not acceptable, in fact they are alarming and shameful.

Later you speak to several of the Elders and confess to them what you are experiencing. They look at you with surprise and sadness. "No!" says one. "That path is forbidden. It leads only to sorrow and death."

"We love you!" says another. "Stay here where it is safe. Conform!"

You determine that you will not go. You shut your ears to the call of the one who spoke from the campfire, and you devote yourself to keeping the rules of the Tribe with all the energy of your soul. On your knees by day and by night you pray to the heavens to make you like the others. You go for days without food to prove how earnest, how worthy you are. Daily you study the holy books. You are called to serve and you serve to perfection. Perhaps you are driven to perfection out of fear, wanting so badly to hide your difference.

But still something within pulls you to the forbidden path.

Then a respected member of the Tribe, who claims to have special knowledge, tells you that he can repair the damage that made you different in the first place, and you can be like everyone else, which is what God wants for you. You put yourself in his care for a very long time, and afterwards, when you are still quite different, you feel worse than ever and you do not believe that is what God wants for you.

"Still," you promise yourself. "I will stay strong no matter what."

Step Four

MEETING
WITH THE
MENTOR

But despite your every effort, you continue to feel different and a strong force pulls you to the new path. "Why is this happening?" you plead in every prayer.

You are much too young to understand, but the Wise One who singled you out whispers, "There is hidden wisdom here. The Great Father and Mother create some that we call 'Two Spirit.' They see the world differently. They bridge gaps, are walkers between worlds. They have a special place as shamans, as artists, as healers to a wound that the Tribe doesn't even know is there."

"Do I have to?" you plead.

"You are called. You can say 'Yes' and walk this path with dignity and joy or you can say 'No' and walk it with fear and pain. But you must walk this path. If you lie to yourself and to others and say, 'I am not different, I am just like everyone else,' you will bring sickness to yourself and to the Tribe. But if you accept the call and succeed in the Hero's journey, you will find the reward, the Elixir. And then the path will become very clear."

"What is the Elixir?" you ask.

The Wise One looks deep into your eyes. "It is a substance capable of curing all ills. And your Tribe is very much in need of it now."

Joseph Campbell:

You Seekers, fearful at the brink of adventure, seek out those who have gone before. You learn the secret lore of watering holes, game trails, and berry patches, and what badlands, quicksand, and monsters to avoid. An old one scratches a map in the dirt, presses something into your hand, a magic gift, a potent talisman that will protect and guide you on the quest. Now you can set out with lighter hearts and greater confidence, for you take with you the collected wisdom of the Home Tribe.

Yes, you remember now. Your ancestors set out for a new land. They sailed oceans, and then step by step they traveled plains. They were reviled, but they pressed on to create a new life. The talisman of their blood is within you. Their courage can be your guide.

And you have been assured since you were small that the Spirit of God abandons no one.

Step Five

CROSSING THE
THRESHOLD

You watch and wait. Maybe if you just lie low you won't be noticed and this Seeker thing will fade away. But then--

You fall in love for the first time!

Suddenly you know what the songs are about. In the crowd you can see only one, and you look at the one in amazement. Just to be in the presence of the one makes real all of the cliches. Adoration. Desire. You are alive like never before. You understand for the first time why it is not good to be alone.

The romance does not last. In fact, it ends badly. But you are forever changed. You have had a taste of something wonderful and the yearning will be with you forever.

The guardians of the threshold stand before you. They hold up one hand that says, "Stop!" They beckon with another hand that says, "Come!"

You are confused, and you remember the Garden of Eden. "Do not partake of the fruit. Do partake of the fruit."

"I am not sure how this will end," you say to yourself, "but there is no question now. Part of my identity is that I am a homosexual human being and it feels right to me. And what I want more than anything is to contribute my special gifts and to create a loving relationship with a partner, with one who is the choice of my heart."

Joseph Campbell:

It's difficult to pull away from everything you know, but with a deep breath you go on, taking the plunge into the abyss of the unknown. There is no turning back now; the adventure has begun for good or ill.

Some members of the Tribe send you off with an embrace, but many in the Tribe turn away, sad or angry or confused or repulsed. Even your own family is divided. You can hardly bear to see the pain on faces that you have loved so dearly.

"You are giving up your eternal exaltation!" says your father.

"Leave, before you pollute my children!" cries your sister.

Your mother holds you tight and says, "I don't understand, my child. But I believe in you. Believe in yourself."

"You are listening to Satan," says one of the Elders, "and he will only lead you astray!"

The words wound you deeply and you feel the rising heat of anger. "It is good that I leave the Tribe," you say to yourself. "These are small-minded people. I am the same person I was before I told them of my difference. Why do they condemn me? I am better off without them."

As you go to pack your knapsack with a few precious things, one of the Elders quietly approaches you and says, "You are not the first. We have lost too many like you. There are many great and important things that we have yet to understand. Please help us." He gives you an embrace and you set off on your journey.

"God be with you!" echo some of the voices.

"God will never be with you!" echo others.

Step Six

ENCOUNTER
TESTS,
ALLIES,
ENEMIES

J oseph Campbell:

You Seekers are in shock—this new world is so
different from the home you've always known.
Not only are the terrain and the local residents
different, the rules of this place are strange as
they can be. Different things are valued here.
Strange creatures jump out at you! Think fast!
Don't eat that, it could be poison!

This is the world of the Shadow, filled with
traps and barricades. Who can you trust? What
is real and what is a hollow and painted imita-

tion? At every corner people are selling their wares.

Here is a shop that will make you look and dress really, really cool. If you look and dress and sound really, really cool, perhaps you won't feel different after all.

Here is someone who has a potion that will take away the pain of being different and make you feel awesome. Is it the promised Elixir? You taste it, and you learn something: feeling great for a moment and terrible for many moments cannot be right.

Here is a shop that sells films of stories and scenes that will show you how love is done. In fact, even after your lovers leave, these stories and scenes will be there for you always, and they will become more powerful and appealing than uncertain reality.

You feel new parts of yourself emerging, selfish and materialistic parts that you don't like. This is not what you came out for!

You ask about the men you see who are sick, some dying on the sidewalks, and you are told they didn't stay safe, but you will be fine if you just stay safe.

You make a friend who promises to love you forever, and you wake up with your knapsack stolen and with bloody wounds.

Someone you would never have chosen for a friend shows up with bandages and food and with most of your precious possessions. You are relieved and grateful, and she becomes an ally on the path.

Another Seeker who seems to have the same goals appears and he also becomes an ally. And another. And another. Each is driven by a desire for something more than exists in this part of the new world. Your band of Seekers, comrades now, looks toward the horizon, toward the promised land.

Step Seven

APPROACH
TO THE
INMOST CAVE

Joseph Campbell:

A new perception of yourself and others is forming ... . You are refreshed and armed with more knowledge about the nature and habits of the game you're hunting. You're ready to press on to the heart of the new world where the greatest treasures are guarded by the greatest fears ... . Soon you will be ready to enter the Inmost Cave.

There!—across a divide—a glimpse of that new place, a glimpse of those treasures! Seekers just like you–different just like you–happy, creative, peaceful, giving their special gifts to the Larger Tribe. And many of them sharing with another that remarkable tenderness and care, that sweet, joyful pleasure you remember. Oh, to be there! The challenges of the past have strengthened you and you know you are prepared.

You and your comrades hurry toward the border.

"Stop!" The Border Guard shouts. "There is no way to go across. You must go through."

"Through?" you ask.

The Guard steps aside to reveal a dark opening. "Through the cave. The Inmost Cave."

You look to your comrades. They nod, determined, ready to move.

"Alone," says the Guard. "One by one. Some

of you may not survive." A terrifying howl comes from within the cave. "It is possible to turn back now," says the Guard.

Two of your comrades grow pale. The howl comes again. Without a word, they turn around and begin the journey back.

"No!" you call. But they are gone.

You study the dark cave. "How long does it take?" you ask the Guard.

"To some it is less than the turn of a sun and a moon," comes the reply. "To others, it can be many years. And some," he continues sadly, "some come out–never."

You breathe deeply, and then you step forward. You know you are on the edge of life and death. But you step forward.

Step Eight

THE
SUPREME
ORDEAL

J oseph Campbell:

*Seeker, enter the Immost Cave ... the way
grows narrow and dark. You must go alone on
hands and knees and you feel the earth press
close around you. You can hardly breathe. Suddenly you find yourself face to face with a tow-
ering figure, a menacing Shadow composed of
all your doubts and fears. It is Death that now
stares back at you.*

"You," says the Shadow with loathing in his
voice. "There is something very, very wrong with

you. At best you are a mistake and at worst you are an abomination. You would be better off not to exist than to be what you are."

Where did you hear those words before? Yes, one of the Elders spoke them to you back home. The Shadow speaks again and his words echo from every direction in the dark cave.

"Your path is the Path of Satan. You will lose your eternal exaltation. Wickedness never was happiness!" Hours pass, or is it days? All the condemning words you heard for years bounce from wall to wall and carve themselves into your mind. "The desires you feel are not of God. If you act on them you are committing an abomination."

The Shadow holds out a sword. "It is better to lose your life than to shame your family, your Tribe and to lose your eternal soul. End your life now before you reap damnation and heap shame on those who love you!"

You put your hands over your ears, but still the words pierce. "Pervert ... Sin against nature ... Embarrassing ... Detestable ... No place for you in the Kingdom ... No place for you!"

The Shadow thrusts the sword closer to you and says, "End it all now!"

You fall to your knees as you have hundreds of times, and you cry out as you have hundreds of times.

"Dear God, I have to know. Am I a mistake? Are my deepest desires an abomination in your sight? Is there no place for me in the Plan?" Weeping, you remain on your knees.

And then you hear another Voice. "The answers," it says, "are inside of you. Listen to the Spirit within as I ask you this. Are you a mistake?"

You listen, then you speak. "No," you say softly. "I am not."

"Is the love you yearn for an abomination?"

Again you listen for an answer within. "No. It is not."

"With the partner you yearn for, would you be capable of kindness, patience, sacrifice, fidelity and joy?"

"I would."

"Seize the sword," says the Voice.

You understand. You grasp the instrument of death, its blade glittering, and you lift it high, poised at the Shadow.

"Strike now!" you hear.

"No!" cries the Shadow. "I am the one who speaks the truth!"

They are with you now, your ancestors who

set out for a new land, your friends and family in the home Tribe who told you to believe in yourself. Their courage speaks. "Strike now!"

Moving closer, the Shadow cries out, "Pitiful freak! There is no place for you and no reward but misery! End it all now!"

You feel tears in your eyes and the light that was always within you grows so bright and warm you believe your heart will burst. The words come now without effort, with clarity and strength. "There is a place for me. I am Light. And I am God's beloved Child."

And then, with a force you did not know you had, you strike your fears. One thrust, and with a scream the Shadow splits and dissolves into smoke, revealing an opening on the other side of the cave. The brightness of blue sky appears.

You run.

Step Nine

REWARD

J oseph Campbell:

You Seekers look at one another with growing
smiles. You faced death, tasted it, and yet lived.
From the depths of terror you suddenly shoot up
to victory. Strangely quiet now, in the leaping
shadows, you remember those who didn't make
it, and you notice something. You've changed.
Part of you has died and something new has
been born. You and the world will never seem
the same.

Reborn. That's what it feels like! You look at
the other Seekers who have emerged from the

Inmost Cave. Their Supreme Ordeal must have been very much like your own because as you look into their eyes you see—not the confusion, not the fear, not the selfish hunger or the pain or the loneliness that you felt and saw in the eyes of so many on the other side of the divide.

In these eyes you see peace, you see confidence, you see enthusiasm, even joy! They know who they are and know that they have an honored place in the Plan. These Seekers have emerged as men and women unbroken, and you have a sudden thought–perhaps one of them is a person with whom you could create joy for a lifetime.

Around the campfire now, you swap stories of the time before, of Tribes and families. When you meet several from your own Mormon Tribe, you can hardly believe it, for you felt you were the only one! You show scars and you comfort one another. You commemorate those who did not make it through the Supreme Ordeal, those who used the sword upon themselves, those who limped broken back to the sad world between the Tribe and the Cave. But mostly you celebrate. You are the ones who not only can survive, but who can thrive.

The songs have been sung, the stories have been told, and you lie down close to the fire dreaming of happy times to come.

With the first ray of morning, a Voice brings you back to this world. The Wise One who spoke to you so long ago speaks again.

Step Ten

THE
ROAD BACK

J oseph Campbell:

Wake up, Seekers! Remember why you came out here in the first place! People back home are starving and it's urgent, now that you've recovered from the ordeal, that you load up your knapsacks with food and treasure and head for home.

"Head for home?" you ask incredulously. "I left home because I was not welcome there. Many there said things that hurt me. Why would I head for home?"

• 61 •

The Wise One smiles and replies, "Whether you do it physically or in your heart, you must make peace with the Tribe you were born to. And they must make peace with you. The Light that came to you in the Inmost Cave, the Light that showed you who you really are and showed that there is a perfect place for you in creation's Plan—that Light is meant for the Tribe as well as for you."

"I can bring Light to my Tribe?" you ask.

The Wise One nods. "No learning is for yourself alone. It is for all."

Reluctantly you pick up your knapsack and turn in the direction of home.

Step Eleven

RESURRECTION

W ait!" says the Wise One.

Joseph Campbell:

You have been to the land of Death, and you look like death itself. If you march back into the village without purifying and cleansing yourselves, you may bring death back with you. The trick is to keep the wisdom of the Ordeal, while getting rid of its bad effects. You must undergo one final sacrifice before rejoining the tribe. Your warrior self must die so you can be reborn as an innocent into the group.

"What does that mean?" you ask.

"You must forgive. You must be grateful for the good things given you by the Tribe and your family. You must hold no resentment or it will poison your heart. You must be able to look at all who harmed you and say, 'I forgive you, for you knew not what you did.' And then you must teach them the Truth of who you really are."

"Teach them? How?"

"You must shine. The Light that you found in the Inmost Cave–can you give it to them? Can you shine even if they still believe that your difference is a defect and your love is a sin?"

You think for a moment. "Yes. I can."

"Can you shine even if you are disappointed in your quest for a partner?"

Again you consider. "I believe I can. I want to."

The Wise One smiles. "Then I think you have found the Elixir and are ready to share it."

The Elixir. You had forgotten. "I have it?" you ask. "The substance that can cure all ills– what is it?"

"The Elixir is Love, always and only Love. Tell me. Do you have it?"

You feel the Light in your heart grow brighter and you know that indeed it is Love and that it will always be there. Love for life, for all, love for yourself. You smile. "I do," you say.

"Do you still have the sword?" asks the Wise One.

"I do."

"Throw it away," he says. "You must go forward unarmed."

You lift the sword and fling it into the tall trees.

Step Twelve

RETURN WITH
THE ELIXIR

You and your comrades walk together toward home. Here and there some veer off to a different path, as their home is not your home. At last you and the others who are children of the Mormon Tribe see its special village ahead of you. You thought you would be frightened at the thought of return, but you are not.

Word spreads that the outcasts have returned. Those who have been sending loving prayers and calling angels to be with you run out first and throw open their arms. Your mother kisses you and says, "In my heart you have never been away." Friends and other family crowd around you.

"You are different," says one.

"I am," you say. "That is why I had to leave."

"No," the friend responds. "This difference is one that makes me forget the other difference."

You smile, for you understand.

Then the Elders come, along with your father who had cautioned you against the loss of your eternal soul. "Why are you here?" asks one of the Elders suspiciously.

"This is home," you reply. "I may stay or I may not, but I am here."

Your father looks at you as if you are a marvel. And then you are circled in his embrace.

You take a deep breath and feel the assurance of the Light within you. You look around at your comrades. You have all traveled much the same terrain, but you have arrived at different points with different experiences and different decisions.

You study them now, these who have become so dear to you.

Those who are in partnerships. They have the Elixir—you can tell by the way they speak and the way they regard one another and the joy that follows them.

The one who married in the way the Tribe had told him was the only way, who went through the dark night of pain and emerged to restructure his relationships to allow more joy for all—he has the Elixir. You can tell by the way he relates to his former spouse and is committed to his children.

The one who also married in the traditional way, hoping for a miracle that never came. She chose between two sacrifices and remains with the family she created. You observe that she too has the Elixir—there is peace in her eyes, and self-assurance and respect. A different kind of miracle.

The one who chose not to search for a partner—and the one whose searching was unsuccessful—they stand alone. But they too have the Elixir, and they share it happily and generously, serving and shining in the lives of those they meet.

And there is you, confident, capable, and grateful.

All of you are Heroes. You survived the pitfalls of the strange new world. You claimed your own Light in the Inmost Cave. You purified yourselves and forgave and came home with the Elixir. You know who you are and you will live and love without apology. This is the way you share the Elixir, the bright Light of Love that transcends judgment and whose source is God. You may or may not stay with the Tribe, but the Tribe is richer for your gifts.

Joseph Campbell:

The Seekers come home at last, purged, purified, and bearing the fruits of your journey. You share the nourishment and treasure among the Home Tribe. A circle has been closed, you can feel it. You can see that your struggles on the Road of Heroes have brought new life to the land, and as it ends it brings deep healing, wellness, and wholeness to the world. The Seekers have come Home.

Then you look around at your Tribe and, to your surprise, you now see in the eyes of many that you had judged as small-minded something you did not notice before. They had been on a journey that you knew nothing about, a challenging and sacred journey they were also called to by a Wise One.

Some of them had been through their own Supreme Ordeal and had emerged from the Inmost Cave as Heroes with the Light of Love and brought it home to share, and you had been warmed by it and had not even known!

Then a new and unexpected thought—is it possible that all, all are Heroes in embryo?

You look into the faces of some of the Elders of the Tribe who have been studying you—the one who bravely spoke to you before you left, and even many of the others—and you see something remarkable—the look of the Seeker.

You can't know for sure, but it feels as if they are putting down an inner burden and hearing an inner Voice and responding, "Yes. The ancestors said this is the place, but the place is very large and the journey is never done."

About the Author

Carol Lynn Pearson is a fourth-generation, active member of the Mormon Tribe. Part of her own path as a Seeker is told in her autobiographical *Goodbye, I Love You*, the story of her marriage to a gay man, Gerald Pearson, who insisted on publishing her first book and whose life made her a reluctant traveler on a very fruitful journey.

For many years Carol Lynn has tirelessly worked toward ending the collision between religion and homosexuality. Among her contributions are a stage play, *Facing East*, the story of a Mormon couple dealing with the suicide of their gay son, and *No More Goodbyes: Circling the Wagons around Our Gay Loved Ones*. Her writing shows an equal commitment to women's issues, working toward the transformation of patriarchy into partnership.

She is the mother of four grown children and lives in Walnut Creek, California. This book and other of her works are available at her website, www.clpearson.com.